50 Rise and Crumb Recipes

By: Kelly Johnson

Table of Contents

- Freshly Baked Sourdough
- Cinnamon Rolls
- Buttermilk Biscuits
- Brioche Buns
- Focaccia with Rosemary
- Banana Bread
- Soft Dinner Rolls
- Challah Bread
- Croissants
- Pretzels
- Soft Pizza Dough
- Cinnamon Swirl Bread
- English Muffins
- Garlic Knots
- Cornbread
- Naan
- Bagels

- Whole Wheat Bread
- Rye Bread
- Pita Bread
- Apple Cinnamon Scones
- Olive Bread
- Lemon Zucchini Bread
- Honey Wheat Rolls
- Pain de Mie
- Sweet Potato Biscuits
- Pain au Chocolat
- Hot Cross Buns
- Pain Complet (Whole Wheat French Bread)
- Rye and Caraway Seed Bread
- Rustic Ciabatta
- Gluten-Free Sourdough
- Zaatar Bread
- Red Velvet Cake with Cream Cheese Frosting
- Sourdough Pancakes
- Pumpkin Bread

- Parker House Rolls
- Oatmeal Bread
- Biscuit Shortcakes
- Almond Croissants
- French Baguettes
- Pretzel Rolls
- Sweet Brioche Rolls
- Honeycomb Loaf
- Chocolate Chip Muffins
- Milk Bread
- Apricot and Almond Danish
- Churros with Chocolate Sauce
- Whole Grain Pita
- Peach Cobber with Biscuit Topping

Freshly Baked Sourdough

Tangy, crusty, and chewy – a classic that never goes out of style.

Ingredients:

- 1 cup sourdough starter
- 1 1/2 cups warm water
- 4 cups bread flour
- 1 1/2 tsp salt

Instructions:

1. Mix starter, water, and flour until dough forms.
2. Knead for 10 minutes, then let rise until doubled (about 4 hours).
3. Shape dough and let it rise again (2 hours).
4. Bake in a preheated oven at 450°F with steam for 30-40 minutes.
5. Cool and slice!

Cinnamon Rolls

Soft, sweet, and comforting with layers of gooey cinnamon sugar.
Ingredients:

- 1 cup milk
- 1/4 cup butter
- 2 1/4 tsp yeast
- 3 cups flour
- 1/2 cup sugar
- 1/2 tsp salt
- 1 tbsp cinnamon
- 1/2 cup brown sugar

Instructions:

1. Heat milk and butter; mix with yeast and sugar. Let rise.
2. Add flour, salt, and knead until smooth. Let rise.
3. Roll dough, spread cinnamon filling, and roll up. Slice into rolls.
4. Let rise, then bake at 375°F for 20 minutes.
5. Glaze with icing and enjoy!

Buttermilk Biscuits

Flaky, buttery, and melt-in-your-mouth delicious.

Ingredients:

- 2 cups flour
- 1 tbsp baking powder
- 1/2 tsp baking soda
- 1 tsp salt
- 6 tbsp cold butter
- 3/4 cup buttermilk

Instructions:

1. Mix dry ingredients. Cut in butter until crumbly.
2. Add buttermilk and stir until dough forms.
3. Roll out and cut into rounds. Bake at 425°F for 12-15 minutes.
4. Serve warm with butter or jam!

Brioche Buns

Soft, buttery, and perfect for sandwiches or burgers.

Ingredients:

- 1/2 cup milk
- 1/2 cup water
- 3 tbsp sugar
- 2 1/4 tsp yeast
- 4 cups flour
- 1/4 cup butter, softened
- 1 egg

Instructions:

1. Combine warm milk, water, sugar, and yeast. Let bloom.
2. Add flour, butter, and eggs. Knead until smooth. Let rise.
3. Shape dough into buns and let rise again.
4. Bake at 375°F for 20 minutes. Cool and serve!

Focaccia with Rosemary

Herb-infused, golden, and crispy on the outside, soft on the inside.

Ingredients:

- 3 cups flour
- 1 cup water
- 2 tsp yeast
- 1/4 cup olive oil
- 2 tsp salt
- Fresh rosemary, chopped

Instructions:

1. Mix flour, water, yeast, and salt to form dough.
2. Let rise, then spread into a baking pan.
3. Drizzle with olive oil and top with rosemary.
4. Bake at 400°F for 20-25 minutes. Serve warm!

Banana Bread

Moist and flavorful with a hint of sweetness.

Ingredients:

- 2 ripe bananas
- 1/2 cup butter, softened
- 1 cup sugar
- 2 eggs
- 2 cups flour
- 1 tsp baking soda
- 1/4 tsp salt

Instructions:

1. Mash bananas and mix with butter, sugar, and eggs.
2. Add flour, baking soda, and salt. Stir to combine.
3. Pour into greased loaf pan.
4. Bake at 350°F for 60-65 minutes.

Soft Dinner Rolls

Fluffy, buttery rolls perfect for family meals.

Ingredients:

- 3 cups flour
- 1 tbsp sugar
- 1 tsp salt
- 1 package yeast
- 1 cup warm milk
- 2 tbsp butter

Instructions:

1. Combine warm milk, sugar, and yeast. Let rise.
2. Add flour, salt, and butter. Knead and let rise.
3. Shape into rolls, let rise, and bake at 375°F for 15-20 minutes.

Challah Bread

A rich, sweet, and tender braided bread with a golden finish.

Ingredients:

- 4 cups flour
- 1 tbsp yeast
- 1/4 cup sugar
- 1 cup warm water
- 1/2 cup oil
- 3 eggs

Instructions:

1. Mix warm water, sugar, and yeast; let rise.
2. Add flour, oil, and eggs. Knead and let rise.
3. Braid dough and let rise again.
4. Bake at 350°F for 30-35 minutes.

Croissants

Flaky, buttery layers that are perfect for breakfast.
Ingredients:

- 2 cups flour
- 1 tbsp sugar
- 1 tsp salt
- 1 tbsp yeast
- 3/4 cup cold butter
- 1/2 cup milk

Instructions:

1. Mix dry ingredients and milk. Knead into dough and let rest.
2. Roll dough, layer with butter, and fold. Chill and repeat folding.
3. Shape into croissants and let rise.
4. Bake at 400°F for 15-20 minutes.

Pretzels

Soft, chewy, and salty — perfect with mustard or cheese sauce.

Ingredients:

- 2 1/4 tsp yeast
- 1 1/2 cups warm water
- 4 cups flour
- 1 tbsp sugar
- 1 tsp salt
- Baking soda for boiling

Instructions:

1. Mix yeast, water, sugar, and salt to form dough.
2. Let rise, then shape into pretzels.
3. Boil in baking soda water for 30 seconds.
4. Bake at 400°F for 10-12 minutes. Top with salt.

Soft Pizza Dough

Perfectly soft, chewy, and easy to work with for all your pizza cravings.

Ingredients:

- 1 1/2 cups warm water
- 1 tsp sugar
- 2 1/4 tsp yeast
- 3 1/2 cups flour
- 1 tsp salt
- 2 tbsp olive oil

Instructions:

1. Combine warm water, sugar, and yeast. Let sit for 5-10 minutes until foamy.
2. Add flour, salt, and olive oil. Knead until smooth.
3. Let rise in a warm place for 1-2 hours.
4. Roll out the dough, add your favorite toppings, and bake at 475°F for 10-15 minutes.

Cinnamon Swirl Bread

Sweet, soft, and filled with a swirl of cinnamon sugar – perfect for breakfast or dessert!

Ingredients:

- 2 1/2 cups flour
- 1 tbsp sugar
- 1 tsp salt
- 2 1/4 tsp yeast
- 1 cup warm milk
- 1/4 cup butter
- 1/2 cup sugar (for cinnamon filling)
- 2 tbsp cinnamon

Instructions:

1. Mix warm milk, sugar, and yeast. Let rise.
2. Add flour, salt, butter, and knead. Let rise for 1 hour.
3. Roll out dough, sprinkle with cinnamon-sugar, and roll up.
4. Let rise for another hour, then bake at 350°F for 30-35 minutes.

English Muffins

Soft, airy, and perfect for breakfast sandwiches or toasting with jam.

Ingredients:

- 1 cup warm milk
- 1 tbsp sugar
- 2 tsp yeast
- 3 cups flour
- 1 tsp salt
- Cornmeal for dusting

Instructions:

1. Mix warm milk, sugar, and yeast, and let sit for 5 minutes.
2. Add flour and salt, knead into dough. Let rise for 1 hour.
3. Roll out dough and cut into rounds. Let rise again.
4. Cook on a hot griddle over medium heat for 5-6 minutes per side.

Garlic Knots

Soft, garlicky, and buttery – perfect for serving with pasta or as a snack.

Ingredients:

- 1 pizza dough recipe (or store-bought)
- 4 cloves garlic, minced
- 4 tbsp butter, melted
- 1 tsp dried oregano
- Salt to taste

Instructions:

1. Preheat oven to 400°F.
2. Cut dough into strips and tie into knots.
3. Place on a baking sheet and brush with melted butter, garlic, oregano, and salt.
4. Bake for 12-15 minutes until golden brown.

Cornbread

Sweet, moist, and perfectly crumbly – a classic side dish for chili or barbecue.

Ingredients:

- 1 cup cornmeal
- 1 cup flour
- 1/4 cup sugar
- 1 tbsp baking powder
- 1/2 tsp salt
- 1 cup buttermilk
- 1/4 cup butter, melted
- 2 eggs

Instructions:

1. Preheat oven to 375°F. Grease a baking dish.
2. Mix cornmeal, flour, sugar, baking powder, and salt.
3. Stir in buttermilk, melted butter, and eggs.
4. Pour into prepared pan and bake for 20-25 minutes.

Naan

Soft, fluffy, and perfect for dipping into curry or wrapping around grilled meats.

Ingredients:

- 1 cup warm water
- 1 tbsp sugar
- 2 tsp yeast
- 3 cups flour
- 1 tsp salt
- 2 tbsp yogurt
- 2 tbsp butter, melted

Instructions:

1. Mix warm water, sugar, and yeast. Let sit for 5 minutes.
2. Add flour, salt, yogurt, and knead. Let rise for 1 hour.
3. Roll out dough and cook in a hot skillet for 2-3 minutes per side.

Bagels

Chewy, dense, and delicious – perfect for breakfast with cream cheese or smoked salmon.

Ingredients:

- 1 1/2 cups warm water
- 1 tbsp sugar
- 2 tsp yeast
- 4 cups flour
- 1 tsp salt
- 1 tbsp vegetable oil

Instructions:

1. Mix warm water, sugar, and yeast. Let sit for 5 minutes.
2. Add flour and salt, knead into dough. Let rise for 1 hour.
3. Shape dough into bagels and boil in water with sugar for 2 minutes per side.
4. Bake at 425°F for 20-25 minutes.

Whole Wheat Bread

Nutty, hearty, and full of flavor – a perfect healthier bread option.

Ingredients:

- 3 cups whole wheat flour
- 1 1/2 cups warm water
- 2 tbsp honey
- 1 tbsp yeast
- 1 1/2 tsp salt

Instructions:

1. Mix warm water, honey, and yeast. Let rise for 5 minutes.
2. Add flour and salt, knead into dough. Let rise for 1-2 hours.
3. Shape into loaf and bake at 375°F for 25-30 minutes.

Rye Bread

Earthy, flavorful, and slightly tangy – perfect for sandwiches or paired with cheese.
Ingredients:

- 2 cups rye flour
- 2 cups all-purpose flour
- 1 tbsp yeast
- 1 tbsp sugar
- 1 1/2 cups warm water
- 1 tsp salt

Instructions:

1. Mix warm water, sugar, and yeast. Let sit for 5 minutes.
2. Add flours and salt, knead into dough. Let rise for 1-2 hours.
3. Shape dough into a loaf and bake at 375°F for 30-35 minutes.

Pita Bread

Soft, fluffy, and perfect for filling with all your favorite ingredients.

Ingredients:

- 1 1/2 cups warm water
- 1 tbsp sugar
- 2 1/4 tsp yeast
- 3 cups flour
- 1 tsp salt

Instructions:

1. Mix warm water, sugar, and yeast. Let sit for 5 minutes.
2. Add flour and salt, knead into dough. Let rise for 1-2 hours.
3. Roll dough into rounds and bake at 475°F for 5-7 minutes until puffy.

Apple Cinnamon Scones

Flaky, buttery scones with a sweet apple and cinnamon twist.

Ingredients:

- 2 cups flour
- 1/4 cup sugar
- 1 tbsp baking powder
- 1/2 tsp cinnamon
- 1/2 tsp salt
- 1/2 cup cold butter
- 1/2 cup milk
- 1/2 cup diced apples (peeled and cored)
- 1 egg (for egg wash)

Instructions:

1. Preheat oven to 375°F.
2. Combine dry ingredients, then cut in cold butter until crumbly.
3. Add milk and apples, mix until dough forms.
4. Turn dough onto a floured surface, roll out to 1-inch thick. Cut into wedges.
5. Place on baking sheet, brush with egg wash. Bake for 20-25 minutes.

Olive Bread

Savory, rich bread with a burst of olive flavor.

Ingredients:

- 3 cups flour
- 1 tbsp yeast
- 1 tbsp sugar
- 1 1/2 cups warm water
- 2 tbsp olive oil
- 1/2 cup green olives (chopped)
- 1/2 cup black olives (chopped)
- 1 tsp salt

Instructions:

1. Dissolve sugar and yeast in warm water and let sit for 5 minutes.
2. Mix flour, salt, and olive oil. Add the yeast mixture and knead for 5-8 minutes.
3. Add olives and knead until evenly distributed.
4. Let dough rise for 1-2 hours. Punch down and shape into a loaf.
5. Bake at 375°F for 30-35 minutes until golden.

Lemon Zucchini Bread

Moist, flavorful bread with a tangy lemon and veggie twist.

Ingredients:

- 2 cups flour
- 1 tsp baking powder
- 1/2 tsp baking soda
- 1/2 tsp salt
- 1 tsp cinnamon
- 1/2 cup sugar
- 1/2 cup brown sugar
- 2 eggs
- 1/2 cup vegetable oil
- 1 tsp vanilla extract
- 1 1/2 cups grated zucchini
- Zest of 1 lemon
- 2 tbsp lemon juice

Instructions:

1. Preheat oven to 350°F. Grease a loaf pan.
2. Mix dry ingredients in one bowl. Beat eggs and sugars in another.
3. Add oil, vanilla, lemon zest, and juice to wet ingredients.

4. Stir in zucchini. Gradually add dry ingredients to wet and mix.

5. Pour into pan and bake for 55-60 minutes.

Honey Wheat Rolls

Soft, slightly sweet, and fluffy rolls with whole wheat flour and honey.

Ingredients:

- 2 cups all-purpose flour
- 1 cup whole wheat flour
- 1/4 cup honey
- 1 tbsp yeast
- 1 tsp salt
- 1 cup warm water
- 2 tbsp butter

Instructions:

1. Mix warm water, yeast, and honey. Let sit for 5 minutes.
2. Add flour and salt, mix into dough. Knead for 5-7 minutes.
3. Let dough rise for 1 hour. Punch down and shape into rolls.
4. Let rise again for 30 minutes, then bake at 375°F for 12-15 minutes.

Pain de Mie

Soft, tender, and slightly sweet French bread, perfect for sandwiches.

Ingredients:

- 3 cups flour
- 2 tbsp sugar
- 1 tsp salt
- 1 tbsp yeast
- 1 cup warm milk
- 1/4 cup butter

Instructions:

1. Dissolve yeast in warm milk and let sit for 5 minutes.
2. Mix flour, sugar, and salt. Add yeast mixture and butter, knead for 8-10 minutes.
3. Let rise for 1-2 hours. Punch down, shape into a loaf, and place in a loaf pan.
4. Let rise again for 30 minutes, then bake at 375°F for 25-30 minutes.

Sweet Potato Biscuits

Flaky, buttery biscuits with the comforting sweetness of sweet potatoes.

Ingredients:

- 2 cups flour
- 1 tbsp baking powder
- 1/2 tsp salt
- 1/4 cup cold butter
- 1/2 cup mashed sweet potato
- 1/2 cup milk

Instructions:

1. Preheat oven to 400°F.
2. Mix flour, baking powder, and salt. Cut in cold butter until crumbly.
3. Add sweet potato and milk, mix until dough forms.
4. Turn out onto a floured surface, roll out, and cut into rounds.
5. Bake for 12-15 minutes.

Pain au Chocolat

Flaky, buttery croissants filled with rich chocolate.

Ingredients:

- 2 cups flour
- 1 tbsp sugar
- 1 tsp salt
- 1 tbsp yeast
- 3/4 cup cold butter
- 1/2 cup warm milk
- 1 egg
- 4 oz chocolate (chopped)

Instructions:

1. Mix warm milk, yeast, and sugar. Let sit for 5 minutes.
2. Mix flour, salt, and egg, then add yeast mixture. Knead for 8 minutes.
3. Roll out dough, fold in butter, and refrigerate for 1 hour.
4. Roll out dough and cut into squares. Place chocolate in the center.
5. Roll up and bake at 375°F for 20-25 minutes.

Hot Cross Buns

Spicy, fruity buns topped with a signature cross for Easter or any special occasion.

Ingredients:

- 3 cups flour
- 1/4 cup sugar
- 1 tbsp yeast
- 1/2 tsp salt
- 1 tsp cinnamon
- 1/2 cup milk
- 1/4 cup butter
- 2 eggs
- 1/2 cup dried currants or raisins
- 1 tbsp milk (for glaze)
- 1/4 cup powdered sugar (for glaze)

Instructions:

1. Mix warm milk, sugar, and yeast. Let sit for 5 minutes.
2. Add flour, salt, cinnamon, butter, and eggs. Knead for 10 minutes.
3. Let rise for 1-2 hours, then add currants.
4. Shape into buns and let rise for another 30 minutes.
5. Bake at 375°F for 15-18 minutes, then glaze with milk and powdered sugar.

Pain Complet (Whole Wheat French Bread)

Nutty and hearty, this French-style whole wheat bread has a rustic, chewy texture.

Ingredients:

- 3 cups whole wheat flour
- 1 tbsp yeast
- 1 tbsp sugar
- 1 1/2 cups warm water
- 1 tsp salt

Instructions:

1. Mix warm water, sugar, and yeast. Let sit for 5 minutes.
2. Add flour and salt, knead for 10 minutes.
3. Let rise for 1-2 hours, then punch down.
4. Shape into a loaf and let rise again for 30 minutes.
5. Bake at 375°F for 30-35 minutes.

Rye and Caraway Seed Bread

Hearty and aromatic rye bread with the signature crunch of caraway seeds.

Ingredients:

- 1 1/2 cups rye flour
- 1 1/2 cups bread flour
- 1 tbsp caraway seeds
- 1 tbsp sugar
- 1 tsp salt
- 1 tbsp yeast
- 1 1/2 cups warm water
- 2 tbsp olive oil

Instructions:

1. Mix warm water, sugar, and yeast, let sit for 5 minutes.
2. Combine both flours, caraway seeds, and salt. Add the yeast mixture and olive oil.
3. Knead for 10 minutes until smooth.
4. Let rise for 1-2 hours. Punch down and shape into a loaf.
5. Bake at 375°F for 30-35 minutes until golden.

Rustic Ciabatta

Crusty and airy with a chewy interior.

Ingredients:

- 4 cups bread flour
- 1 tsp salt
- 2 tbsp olive oil
- 1 tbsp yeast
- 1 1/2 cups warm water

Instructions:

1. Mix yeast with warm water and let sit for 5 minutes.
2. Add flour, salt, and olive oil. Stir until a dough forms.
3. Knead for 5 minutes, then cover and let rise for 1-2 hours.
4. Punch down, shape into a rustic loaf, and let rise for another hour.
5. Bake at 400°F for 25-30 minutes.

Gluten-Free Sourdough

Deliciously tangy sourdough without the gluten.

Ingredients:

- 2 cups gluten-free flour blend
- 1 tsp salt
- 1 tbsp sugar
- 1 tbsp yeast
- 1 1/2 cups warm water
- 1 tbsp olive oil

Instructions:

1. Combine yeast, warm water, and sugar. Let sit for 5 minutes.
2. Stir in gluten-free flour, salt, and olive oil. Mix until dough forms.
3. Let rise for 1-2 hours, then punch down and shape into a loaf.
4. Let rise for another hour.
5. Bake at 375°F for 30-35 minutes.

Zaatar Bread

A Middle Eastern flatbread topped with aromatic za'atar seasoning.

Ingredients:

- 3 cups flour
- 1 tsp salt
- 1 tbsp sugar
- 1 tbsp yeast
- 1 1/4 cups warm water
- 3 tbsp olive oil
- 2 tbsp za'atar seasoning

Instructions:

1. Mix yeast with warm water and sugar, let sit for 5 minutes.
2. Combine flour and salt, then add the yeast mixture and olive oil.
3. Knead for 10 minutes and let rise for 1-2 hours.
4. Shape dough into a flatbreads, brush with olive oil, and sprinkle with za'atar.
5. Bake at 400°F for 10-12 minutes.

Red Velvet Cake with Cream Cheese Frosting

A moist and rich red velvet cake topped with tangy cream cheese frosting.

Ingredients (Cake):

- 2 1/2 cups all-purpose flour
- 1 1/2 cups sugar
- 1 tsp baking soda
- 1 tsp cocoa powder
- 1 tsp salt
- 1 1/2 cups vegetable oil
- 1 cup buttermilk
- 2 eggs
- 2 tbsp red food coloring
- 1 tsp vanilla extract
- 1 tsp white vinegar

Ingredients (Frosting):

- 8 oz cream cheese, softened
- 1/2 cup unsalted butter, softened
- 4 cups powdered sugar
- 1 tsp vanilla extract

Instructions (Cake):

1. Preheat oven to 350°F. Grease and flour two 9-inch cake pans.

2. Mix dry ingredients. Add wet ingredients and mix until smooth.

3. Divide batter evenly between pans and bake for 25-30 minutes.

4. Let cool completely before frosting.

Instructions (Frosting):

1. Beat cream cheese and butter until smooth.

2. Gradually add powdered sugar and vanilla, beat until fluffy.

3. Frost cooled cakes.

Sourdough Pancakes

Fluffy pancakes with a tangy sourdough twist.

Ingredients:

- 1 cup sourdough starter
- 1 cup flour
- 1 egg
- 1 tbsp sugar
- 1 tsp baking powder
- 1/2 tsp baking soda
- 1/2 cup milk
- 2 tbsp butter, melted

Instructions:

1. Mix all ingredients together until smooth.
2. Heat a skillet over medium heat and grease with butter.
3. Pour batter onto skillet in desired pancake size.
4. Cook until bubbles appear, then flip and cook the other side.

Pumpkin Bread

A warm, spiced bread perfect for fall.

Ingredients:

- 1 1/2 cups flour
- 1 tsp baking soda
- 1/2 tsp baking powder
- 1 tsp cinnamon
- 1/2 tsp nutmeg
- 1/2 tsp salt
- 1 cup pumpkin puree
- 1/2 cup sugar
- 1/2 cup brown sugar
- 2 eggs
- 1/2 cup vegetable oil

Instructions:

1. Preheat oven to 350°F and grease a loaf pan.
2. Mix dry ingredients. In another bowl, whisk eggs, pumpkin, sugars, and oil.
3. Combine both mixtures and pour into loaf pan.
4. Bake for 50-60 minutes.

Parker House Rolls

Soft, buttery rolls with a light and fluffy texture.

Ingredients:

- 1 1/2 cups flour
- 1 tsp salt
- 2 tbsp sugar
- 2 tbsp butter
- 1 tbsp yeast
- 1/2 cup warm milk
- 1 egg

Instructions:

1. Dissolve yeast in warm milk with sugar, let sit for 5 minutes.
2. Combine flour, salt, and butter. Add the yeast mixture and egg, knead for 5 minutes.
3. Let rise for 1 hour, then divide dough into small rolls.
4. Bake at 375°F for 12-15 minutes.

Oatmeal Bread

Nutty and hearty, this oatmeal bread is perfect for sandwiches.

Ingredients:

- 1 1/2 cups rolled oats
- 2 cups flour
- 1 tsp salt
- 1 tbsp sugar
- 2 tbsp yeast
- 1 1/2 cups warm water
- 2 tbsp butter

Instructions:

1. Mix warm water, sugar, and yeast, let sit for 5 minutes.
2. Add oats, flour, salt, and butter, mix into dough.
3. Knead for 8 minutes, then let rise for 1-2 hours.
4. Shape into a loaf and let rise for another 30 minutes.
5. Bake at 375°F for 30-35 minutes.

Biscuit Shortcakes

Flaky and buttery biscuit shortcakes, perfect for strawberry shortcake or other desserts.

Ingredients:

- 2 cups all-purpose flour
- 1/4 cup sugar
- 1 tbsp baking powder
- 1/2 tsp baking soda
- 1/2 tsp salt
- 1/2 cup cold unsalted butter, cubed
- 3/4 cup buttermilk

Instructions:

1. Preheat oven to 400°F. Grease a baking sheet.
2. In a large bowl, mix flour, sugar, baking powder, baking soda, and salt.
3. Cut in cold butter until mixture resembles coarse crumbs.
4. Stir in buttermilk until just combined.
5. Turn dough out onto a floured surface and gently pat it into a rectangle. Fold it over a few times to create layers.
6. Cut dough into rounds and place on the baking sheet.
7. Bake for 12-15 minutes until golden.

Almond Croissants

Flaky, buttery croissants filled with almond paste and topped with sliced almonds.

Ingredients:

- 1 package of croissant dough (or homemade)
- 1/2 cup almond paste
- 1/4 cup powdered sugar
- 2 tbsp butter, softened
- 1 egg, beaten (for egg wash)
- Sliced almonds for topping

Instructions:

1. Preheat oven to 375°F.
2. Roll out croissant dough and cut into triangles.
3. In a bowl, mix almond paste, powdered sugar, and butter until smooth.
4. Spread the almond mixture onto the center of each triangle.
5. Roll the dough up and shape into croissants.
6. Brush with beaten egg and sprinkle with sliced almonds.
7. Bake for 15-18 minutes until golden brown.

French Baguettes

Classic long, thin, and crunchy French baguettes.

Ingredients:

- 4 cups all-purpose flour
- 1 1/2 tsp salt
- 1 tbsp sugar
- 1 tbsp active dry yeast
- 1 1/4 cups warm water
- 1 tbsp olive oil

Instructions:

1. Combine warm water, sugar, and yeast in a bowl. Let sit for 5 minutes.
2. In a large bowl, mix flour and salt. Add the yeast mixture and olive oil, and stir to combine.
3. Knead for 10 minutes, then let rise for 1-2 hours.
4. Punch down dough and shape into two baguettes.
5. Place on a baking sheet and let rise for another 30 minutes.
6. Preheat oven to 475°F, place a pan of water in the bottom of the oven for steam.
7. Bake for 20-25 minutes until golden and crusty.

Pretzel Rolls

Soft, chewy pretzel rolls with a golden brown, salted crust.

Ingredients:

- 3 1/2 cups all-purpose flour
- 1 tbsp sugar
- 2 tsp salt
- 1 tbsp active dry yeast
- 1 1/2 cups warm water
- 1/4 cup baking soda (for boiling)
- Coarse sea salt for topping

Instructions:

1. Dissolve yeast and sugar in warm water, let sit for 5 minutes.
2. Combine flour and salt, then add the yeast mixture. Mix into a dough.
3. Knead for 8-10 minutes, then let rise for 1 hour.
4. Punch down dough, divide into small balls, and let rise for 30 minutes.
5. Bring a pot of water to a boil, add baking soda. Boil each roll for 30 seconds.
6. Place rolls on a baking sheet, sprinkle with coarse sea salt.
7. Bake at 425°F for 12-15 minutes.

Sweet Brioche Rolls

Rich, buttery, and slightly sweet brioche rolls.

Ingredients:

- 2 cups all-purpose flour
- 1/2 cup sugar
- 1 tsp salt
- 2 tsp active dry yeast
- 1/2 cup warm milk
- 1/4 cup butter, softened
- 2 eggs

Instructions:

1. Mix warm milk, sugar, and yeast. Let sit for 5 minutes.
2. Add flour, salt, butter, and eggs to the yeast mixture. Mix until a dough forms.
3. Knead for 8-10 minutes, then let rise for 1-2 hours.
4. Shape dough into rolls and place in a greased pan.
5. Let rise for 30 minutes.
6. Bake at 375°F for 15-20 minutes until golden brown.

Honeycomb Loaf

A soft, airy loaf with a sweet honey flavor.

Ingredients:

- 3 cups bread flour
- 1 tbsp yeast
- 1 tbsp sugar
- 1 tsp salt
- 1/2 cup warm water
- 2 tbsp honey
- 1 tbsp butter, melted

Instructions:

1. Dissolve yeast and sugar in warm water, let sit for 5 minutes.
2. Mix flour and salt in a large bowl, then add yeast mixture, honey, and melted butter.
3. Knead for 10 minutes, then let rise for 1 hour.
4. Punch down the dough, shape it into a loaf, and place in a greased pan.
5. Let rise for 30 minutes.
6. Bake at 350°F for 25-30 minutes.

Chocolate Chip Muffins

Soft, fluffy muffins with melty chocolate chips inside.

Ingredients:

- 2 cups all-purpose flour
- 3/4 cup sugar
- 1 tbsp baking powder
- 1/2 tsp salt
- 1/2 cup unsalted butter, melted
- 1 cup milk
- 2 eggs
- 1 tsp vanilla extract
- 1 1/2 cups semi-sweet chocolate chips

Instructions:

1. Preheat oven to 375°F. Line a muffin tin with paper liners.
2. In a large bowl, mix flour, sugar, baking powder, and salt.
3. In a separate bowl, whisk together melted butter, milk, eggs, and vanilla extract.
4. Add the wet ingredients to the dry ingredients and stir until just combined.
5. Fold in the chocolate chips.
6. Scoop batter into the muffin tin, filling each cup about 3/4 full.
7. Bake for 20-25 minutes, until a toothpick comes out clean.

Milk Bread

Soft, fluffy, and slightly sweet bread with a milky flavor.

Ingredients:

- 3 cups all-purpose flour
- 1/4 cup sugar
- 1 tsp salt
- 1 tbsp active dry yeast
- 1 cup warm milk
- 2 tbsp unsalted butter, melted
- 1 egg

Instructions:

1. Dissolve yeast and sugar in warm milk, let sit for 5 minutes.
2. In a large bowl, combine flour and salt.
3. Add yeast mixture, melted butter, and egg. Stir to combine.
4. Knead the dough for about 8-10 minutes until smooth and elastic.
5. Let the dough rise in a greased bowl for 1-2 hours.
6. Punch down the dough and shape into a loaf. Place in a greased loaf pan.
7. Let it rise for another 30 minutes.
8. Preheat oven to 350°F and bake for 25-30 minutes until golden brown.

Apricot and Almond Danish

Flaky, buttery pastries filled with apricot preserves and almond paste.

Ingredients:

- 1 package puff pastry (thawed)
- 1/2 cup apricot preserves
- 1/2 cup almond paste
- 1 egg (for egg wash)
- Sliced almonds for topping

Instructions:

1. Preheat oven to 375°F. Line a baking sheet with parchment paper.
2. Roll out puff pastry on a lightly floured surface and cut into squares.
3. In a small bowl, combine almond paste with apricot preserves.
4. Place a spoonful of the apricot-almond mixture in the center of each square.
5. Fold the corners of the pastry over to form a pocket or triangle.
6. Brush the pastries with beaten egg and sprinkle with sliced almonds.
7. Bake for 15-20 minutes until golden brown.

Churros with Chocolate Sauce

Fried dough sticks coated in cinnamon sugar and served with a rich chocolate dipping sauce.

Ingredients for Churros:

- 1 cup water
- 2 tbsp unsalted butter
- 1 tbsp sugar
- 1/2 tsp salt
- 1 cup all-purpose flour
- 2 eggs
- 1 tsp vanilla extract
- 1/2 cup sugar (for coating)
- 1 tbsp ground cinnamon

Ingredients for Chocolate Sauce:

- 1/2 cup heavy cream
- 4 oz semi-sweet chocolate, chopped
- 1 tbsp sugar

Instructions:

1. In a saucepan, combine water, butter, sugar, and salt, and bring to a boil.

2. Remove from heat and stir in flour until a dough forms. Let cool for a few minutes.

3. Beat in eggs and vanilla extract until smooth.

4. Heat oil in a deep frying pan.

5. Using a piping bag with a star tip, pipe dough into the hot oil in 4-6 inch strips. Fry until golden brown, then drain on paper towels.

6. In a small bowl, mix sugar and cinnamon. Roll churros in the cinnamon sugar mixture.

7. For the chocolate sauce: Heat heavy cream in a small saucepan until simmering. Pour over chopped chocolate and stir until smooth.

8. Serve churros with chocolate dipping sauce.

Whole Grain Pita

Soft, chewy pita bread made with whole wheat flour for a nutty flavor.

Ingredients:

- 2 cups whole wheat flour
- 1 cup all-purpose flour
- 1 tbsp sugar
- 1 tsp salt
- 1 tbsp active dry yeast
- 1 1/4 cups warm water
- 2 tbsp olive oil

Instructions:

1. Combine warm water, sugar, and yeast. Let sit for 5 minutes until frothy.
2. In a large bowl, combine the whole wheat flour, all-purpose flour, and salt.
3. Add the yeast mixture and olive oil, and stir until a dough forms.
4. Knead dough for 8-10 minutes until smooth.
5. Let rise in a greased bowl for 1-2 hours, until doubled in size.
6. Punch down the dough, divide into 8 portions, and roll into balls.
7. Roll each ball into a circle, about 1/4 inch thick.
8. Preheat a cast-iron skillet over medium-high heat. Cook each pita for 2-3 minutes on each side until puffed up and golden brown.

Peach Cobbler with Biscuit Topping

Sweet, juicy peaches topped with a buttery biscuit crust.

Ingredients for Filling:

- 4 cups fresh or frozen peaches, sliced
- 1/2 cup sugar
- 1 tbsp lemon juice
- 1 tbsp cornstarch

Ingredients for Biscuit Topping:

- 1 1/2 cups all-purpose flour
- 1/4 cup sugar
- 1 tsp baking powder
- 1/2 tsp baking soda
- 1/4 tsp salt
- 1/2 cup cold butter, cubed
- 2/3 cup buttermilk

Instructions:

1. Preheat oven to 375°F.
2. In a bowl, toss peaches with sugar, lemon juice, and cornstarch. Pour into a greased 9x9 baking dish.
3. In a separate bowl, mix flour, sugar, baking powder, baking soda, and salt.

4. Cut in cold butter until the mixture resembles coarse crumbs.

5. Stir in buttermilk to form a dough.

6. Spoon biscuit dough over the peach mixture.

7. Bake for 35-40 minutes until the top is golden and the filling is bubbly.

www.ingramcontent.com/pod-product-compliance
Lightning Source LLC
LaVergne TN
LVHW061949070526
838199LV00060B/4047